How to Speak Wife

I owe a great debt of gratitude to my editorial advisor, Mr. Matthew Sheehy, who has labored countless hours to make my thoughts and my heart clear to my readers. Matthew Sheehy was born in New York City. He graduated from the SUNY College of Environmental Science and Forestry at Syracuse University in 1997 with a B.S. in chemistry. He then attended Duke University in Durham, North Carolina, with the intention of earning a Ph.D. in chemistry. Upon being called to the ministry under the preaching of Dr. Rick Finley at Fellowship Baptist Church, he left Duke University with an M.S. degree and moved to Northwest Indiana. He began attending the First Baptist Church of Hammond, Indiana, and Hyles-Anderson College in 2000. Matthew graduated from Hyles-Anderson in 2003 with a master's degree in pastoral theology. He has served as a Bible teacher and as an academic advisor at Hammond Baptist High School. Matthew and his wife, Amy, are the parents of one child. They now reside in Crown Point, Indiana.

Dedication

Affectionately dedicated to the married couples of First Baptist Church of Hammond. Thank you for striving alongside of me as we lay a foundation for the generation coming after us to build upon.

I love being your shepherd.

1st Printing – March 2010

ISBN: 978-0-9819603-4-0

All Scripture quotations are from the King James Bible.

CREDITS
Project Manager: Dr. Bob Marshall
Assistant: Rochelle Chalifoux
Transcription: Cyndilu Marshall
Page Design and Layout: Linda Stubblefield
Cover Design: Doug Wruck
Proofreading: Rena Fish, Julie Richter,
and Maria Sarver

To order additional books by Dr. Jack Schaap,
please contact:
HYLES PUBLICATIONS
507 State Street
Hammond, Indiana 46320
www.hylespublications.com
e-mail: info@hylespublications.com

About the Author

*D*r. Jack Schaap is the senior pastor of First Baptist Church of Hammond, Indiana, recognized as one of the largest congregations in America. First Baptist Church has the largest children's and teens' ministries in America. He has a B.S., an M.Ed., and a D.D. from Hyles-Anderson College in Crown Point, Indiana.

Pastor Schaap superintends more than 3,000 young people attending five separate, private Christian schools, including one in China and one in Ghana, whose operation is overseen by First Baptist Church. Pastor Schaap is the chancellor of Hyles-Anderson College, a private Bible college which First Baptist Church operates for the purpose of training preachers, missionaries, and Christian educators.

For more than 20 years, he preached 35 yearly meetings to tens of thousands of teenagers. Dr. Schaap is the author of 17 books and several pamphlets.

Dr. Schaap has been married to his wife Cindy since 1979, and they have two adult children who serve in the ministries of First Baptist Church.

Table of Contents

Introduction

Immigration from Mexico is a hot topic in America. Some people argue that if immigrants come from Mexico, then they should learn English instead of trying to change the American culture. This book is not meant to raise the issue of immigration, but the example is similar to a root problem in marriage.

A husband and wife are like foreign immigrants coming to a new land. He comes to the land of Marriage speaking Husband, and she comes to the land of Marriage speaking Wife. The two languages sound similar, but the same words don't always have the same meanings in the two languages. The way a word is said in Husband is not the way it is interpreted in Wife and vice versa. A common expression of concern in the language of Wife might be a challenge to war in the language of Husband.

The differences between the languages of Husband and Wife are like the differences between American and British English. If an Englishwoman said, "I'm going to give Mr. Smith a ring," she would mean that she was going to call Mr. Smith on the telephone. If your wife said, "I'm going to give Mr. Smith a ring," you would

"When men and women agree, it is only in their conclusions; their reasons are always different."

– George Santayana

assume that she was giving him a piece of jewelry that is a symbol of her love and affection for him. You would be angry and jealous; you would worry that she is leaving you. Both ladies used the same words, but the meaning was different because of the culture.

Marriage is above all a representation of the Lord Jesus Christ and His church. If there is one message that the church needs to get across to the world, it is the love of Jesus Who died so men and women can be saved. The message is poorly displayed in many Christian marriages throughout our country. Lost souls misunderstand the Gospel just like people of different languages cannot comprehend each other. Christian couples should be experts at building good marriages; it ought to be second nature. I want you to be exceedingly brilliant when it comes to building a marriage. It takes more than a desire and passion to build a good marriage.

The first step that I want you and your wife to take is the step of understanding each other. Evaluate if you understand your role as a husband by answering the following questions.

- As a husband, do you know the role God made for you to fulfill?
- As a husband, do you have Biblical expectations for yourself and for your wife?
- Do you know what roles God expects your wife to fulfill?
- Do you know how you are supposed to help her fulfill those roles?
- When you are annoyed by statements from your wife, do you truly understand what she is trying to express?
- Do you consider what she is saying from the perspective of her being a woman?

Most husbands haven't considered these questions. Most husbands could not define their

"Keep in mind that the better you understand what you want and why you want it, the better your chances will be of acquiring it."

— Fred Jandt

role or the role of their wife. If a husband cannot define those roles, then he surely does not know how he is to fulfill those roles, nor how to help his wife fulfill her roles. Christians preach to the world, "Be like me," when they don't even know what they are supposed to be. Christian couples should have the most exemplary marriages in the world because they should operate according to God's principles.

"To effectively communicate, we must realize that we are all different in the way we perceive the world and use this understanding as a guide to our communication with others."

— Anthony Robbins

Genesis records the events that occurred when men put their minds together and started building a tower in Babel. God saw that men could build a tower that would "reach unto heaven" because they were on the same page. He defeated their attempts by confounding their language. God knew that if people could not speak the same language, then they could not build something together. Because God chose to confound their language, we could safely conclude that a common language is the great tool to working together.

You and your wife cannot build a great marriage that will "reach unto heaven" until you speak the same language. *How to Speak Wife* is a tool to help you answer some of these vital questions about your role as a husband and your wife's role as your helper. When God saw the work at the tower of Babel, He said, "...*nothing will be restrained from them...*" because they were on the same page speaking the same language. You and your wife could have a powerful marriage where nothing would be restrained from you if you could translate the language of your wife and master the language that you should be speaking as a husband.

CHAPTER ONE

Defining Your Role as a Husband

*A*s you define your role as a husband, it is best to look at the Bible and understand God's intentions for you in this role instead of trying to work through the modern-day mumbo jumbo and the mess that it has created. I will not include all of the Bible verses in this text, but I recommend that you read the first two chapters of Genesis. In this chapter, it is not my desire to give my opinion; it is my desire to expose how the Bible defines your role as a man.

Genesis 1 records that God created everything. Genesis 2 backtracks and gives more information about two particular creations of God: man and the Garden. These two must be important if God bothered to write about them in more detail. The text says that God gave man four things.

1. God gave man life.

Genesis 2:7 tells the story of God's creating Adam. Genesis 2:8-14 tells the story of God's creating the Garden. Verse 8 describes the first relationship between Adam and the Garden. God made the Garden, and He put Adam in that Garden. *"And the L*ORD *God planted a garden eastward in Eden; and there he put the man whom he had formed."* (Genesis 2:8)

2. God gave man a purpose.

Verse 15 ties these two important creations together and defines a man's purpose. *"And the L*ORD *God took the man, and put him into the garden of Eden to dress it and to keep it."* (Genesis 2:15)

Man's role in the Garden was to dress it and to keep it. When the Bible says that Adam dressed the Garden, it means that he worked and served in it. *Webster's 1828 Dictionary* defines *dress* as "to put something in a straight line or order, to put things in order, and specifically, to till or cultivate."

Adam tilled the land and planted seeds in straight rows as we see farmers do today. When the Bible says that Adam kept the Garden, it means that he protected it, guarded it, and generally took care of its needs.

3. God gave man boundaries.

God, your Creator, gives you a role, and He gives you some boundaries as you play that role. God created

Adam, gave Adam a role in the Garden, and He also gave him some boundaries in Genesis 2:16, 17 that define that role.

"And the LORD God commanded the man, saying, Of every tree of the garden thou mayest freely eat: But of the tree of the knowledge of good and evil, thou shalt not eat of it: for in the day that thou eatest thereof thou shalt surely die."

4. God gave man a helper to accomplish his role.

The last point that I want to derive from the Bible is that God created you, gave you a role as a man, gave you boundaries, and He then gave you a helper. God created Adam, gave him a purpose in caring for the Garden, defined his boundaries, and He then gave Eve to be his helper. *"And the LORD God said, It is not good that the man should be alone; I will make him an help meet for him."* (Genesis 2:18)

Roles make people bristle because they feel confined. When I counsel with couples, I define their separate roles as a husband and a wife. Marital problems ultimately occur when either spouse says, "I will not play my role." You will never improve, grow, or heal your marriage until you find contentment and joy in fulfilling the role that God has given to you. The rest of the chapter is devoted to defining your roles as a man. The companion book *How to Speak Husband* teaches your wife the same roles.

ROLE #1:

Man was made to dominate.

Man has a subconscious desire to dominate or control his environment. That is how God fashioned him. Genesis 1:26-28 records that God said that man would have dominion over the earth and that which is therein. Domination is in a man's genes.

Our culture has an increasing emphasis on house-husbands, shared feelings, and mutual respect; there is nothing wrong with those, and I believe in some of those. However politically correct the world becomes, man cannot escape his innate nature to dominate. God put a man in the Garden by himself and said, "Run the show, Adam." Adam was empowered by God to run his environment.

You probably hate when your wife says, "Maybe we should stop for driving directions." That sentence irks you because when you are driving, you are dominating your environment; that environment is your car. Way back when you were in the seed of Adam, God told you to control your environment, so you naturally do not like when your wife tells you how to control the car.

Teenage boys struggle with being accepted as a man by their parents. When you get married, the struggle will return, but this time you will struggle with your wife. In the companion book, I will teach her the areas in life where she should not treat you as a little boy when God made you to be a dominating man.

I love my world of being the pastor of the First Baptist Church of Hammond. People like to offer their advice on how I should do my job. I am kind to them, but deep down I don't want their advice because I am a man and want to dominate the job that God gave me to do.

Men have an attitude that women think is cocky, arrogant, and self-righteous. I call that attitude God's design for a man. You are not supposed to be a jerk, but there is a confidence that you find in saying, "This is my home. This is my house. This is my wife. These are my kids. This is my car, and I like it with the muffler hanging off. It gives me identity. I will fix it when I am good and ready."

Be careful, though, that you don't confuse your desire to dominate with bullheadedness, stupidity, and laziness; they are not God-given rights. Your wife can respect your manliness, but when you add sloth to your manhood, I can't say that I blame her for the problems that might develop.

ROLE #2:
A man must define himself.

A man defines himself by his work. A man is what a man does. When you and your wife were falling in love and got engaged, you reached the peak of your romantic outreach toward your wife. She believed that you would always be so romantic and thoughtful, but romanticism always falls off from that point. At the peak of your romantic output, you were buying rings, setting up elaborate proposals, kneeling in a restaurant, and making a total jerk of yourself in front of a lot of people. You swooned over your wife.

A Proposal of Marriage	
Translation in Wife	*Translation in Husband*
An extremely romantic evening that culminates in the offer to be the object of his affection and desire for decades to come	The moment I obtained permanent companionship and no longer needed to pursue her.

Suppose I had walked up to you at the point when you were just engaged and said, "Sir, what are you going to do with your life?" There is not a man in the world that would have said, "I am going to be a husband." Men do not define themselves by their relationships. Men define themselves by their work.

Suppose I had asked your wife at the same point, "What are you going to do with your life?"

She would have answered, "I am going to be a wife." Women define themselves by their relationships.

You define yourself by your occupation, and I define myself by my occupation. I am a pastor. I am a teacher. I am a counselor. I am an author. My father was a construction worker; he was also a businessman. Our modern era has confused some characteristics of masculinity by mingling the genders and adding titles and ranks to jobs that make us fight to say within, "I'm as good as you are." That idea is modern humanism that needs to be ignored by Bible-believing people.

Regardless of our culture, a man must define himself. He defines himself by his work. Simply put, a man is what a man does.

Role #3:

A man is a protector.

Men have a subconscious desire to protect; they love it. As a husband, you should protect your wife. Men don't just want to protect their family; they also want to protect their neighbor. A man will protect his neighbor's house as aggressively as he would protect his own house; it is an instinct.

If you saw someone being abused or injured, you wouldn't first ask yourself, "Is there any danger to me if I get involved? What will be the repercussions if I help this lady, knowing my wife will be jealous?" You don't care. You jump out of the car, grab a weapon, and beat whatever person or animal is abusing another. Your wife doesn't understand that you are willing to defend anything. It makes her jealous.

You need to use your desire to protect your wife. You should think, "How can I show my wife how I protect her?" The desire to protect is related to the desire to dominate. If someone injures something that is yours, they have stepped on your turf and dominated it. Men don't like that.

ROLE #4:

Men compete to overcome their natural weaknesses.

Men are competitive. There is just something inside of you that says, "I can beat that." However much money you made last year, you would like to make more this year. When you fail, you say, "If it weren't for such and such, I would have made more." Men believe that they are better than what they appear to be. Men are always trying to say, "You don't even know how good I am. In fact, watch me."

The dares are always with the guys and not with the girls. I realize there are some tomboys who can out wrestle their husbands and embarrass them, but that's not typical. When men get together, they don't say, "Hey

Bob, so do you and your wife have a meaningful relationship?" They don't say, "John, how is your boss? Is he dealing with the emotional crisis of his son's leukemia?" We don't talk about those things.

When men get together and talk about themselves, they are quantifying their greatness. If you are a man, you care how many points are on your buck. If your friend got a six-point buck, then you want an eight-point buck. You brag that your shift made the greatest number of widgets in the history of Widgets, Inc. It doesn't matter what you make, what matters is that you are the best at what you do. Men always want to do better and be more productive. That's what we talk about.

When pastors get together, we talk about how our church is doing. We talk about our attendance numbers. When I get together with pastors, none of them have ever initially asked me, "How is your marriage, and how is Mrs. Schaap?" They might ask about my wife eventually, but deep down, we care about production. In fact, if the first question another man asked was "How is Mrs. Schaap?" then I would suspiciously say, "Why do you want to know?"

When your wife talks with another lady, they might genuinely ask each other, "How is your husband? How is the family?" They don't answer that question with a snide remark like, "Why do you want to know?" Instead, one might say, "Let me tell you about it. My husband is having trouble with a little bit of psoriasis, and we are using 'Scalp X.' What do you recommend?" Men don't care about matters like that. We ask other men about their success so that we can then tell them why ours is better.

The Hebrew word for *man* is *adam*, and it means "to lift up and overcome." The very label that God put on His creation was the label of an overcomer. When God made you, He was saying, "Watch this man overcome everything. Watch him go to work." Once God blew breath into Adam's nostrils, Adam went to work.

Proverbs 20:29 says, *"The glory of young men is their strength: and the beauty of old men is the gray head."* Younger men find their glory in their strength and productivity. Older men don't care about their beauty until they are too old to be productive. They still have a mentality to do something great, but men never really get that touchy-feely ability until they have reached the age where most everything doesn't work anymore. Then we are old, and everything seems beautiful to us.

Old men will say, "We sat in our recliners and read old issues of *Reader's Digest* together." Young men don't do that; young men are physically competitive. Grandpas start living vicariously through their grandchildren when they realize that they can't compete physically. Grandfathers want their grandson to go to college on a scholarship. They want their sons and grandsons to excel in areas in which they could not excel. It is very natural and very right, and God designed it that way. Men are competitive.

ROLE #5:
Men develop a big picture.

Men are big-picture people; they focus on what will happen in the future. The entire area of Eden (not just the Garden) was about 500 miles from east to west and about 500 miles north to south. When God told Adam that it was his, I don't think that Adam blinked and thought that the land was too big for him.

As a pastor, I will never think that my church is big enough. It can always get bigger. Your influence at work is never big enough for your manhood. You know that you could always do more, even if the boss doesn't see it.

The gender of a child is determined at conception, but the child does not begin to develop sexual-specific traits until a few weeks and months later. When boys begin to develop their masculine traits in the womb, the right half of the brain begins to enlarge, the left half shrinks, and the cord that connects the two snaps. Because of this, men tend to be dominated by one half of their brain more than the other. Most men are dominated by the right half of their brain, and this half tends to develop the big picture.

The right half of the brain enables us to perform athletically, have dexterity, and perform manual work. It is where we get a competitive edge, logic, and the ability to explain. The left half of the brain enables us to be artistic, poetic, musical, and excel at some of the sciences. Nothing is feminine or masculine about those traits; it is a result of brain development.

A man can learn to develop both sides of his brain, but we generally don't. There is a stereotype of the male musician who is laughed at by the construction worker. The construction worker thinks that the pianist is a wimp. He would like to break the piano in half with his hands. The chiding is often the result of the burly man's embarrassment at his inability to write a poem; he couldn't pronounce Chaucer if he saw it written and couldn't name a poem by the famous poet. The construction worker knows how to swing a hammer, though; he knows how to turn a wrench; he knows how to fix a gutter; he knows how to lay shingles. The point is that men want a big picture. Some of the pictures are dominated by the left brain and some by the right brain. There are different types of big pictures that men may have.

A VACATION	
Translation in Wife	*Translation in Husband*
Seven days of well-planned activity that exclusively includes your husband and children as well as a large quantity of quality time with the family	An annual event where I accomplish arriving so that I can accomplish returning to my normal life.

For women, both halves of the brain are the same size, and there is a connection between the two. This connection is why women are better at having strengths resulting from both the left and right brain. They really are a little more coordinated.

When you go on vacation, you want to wake up at 3:59 a.m., load the car, and take off by 4:00 a.m. You are on a non-stop trip to Orlando. You don't care if the kids have to go to the bathroom. The only reason you'll stop is because the car doesn't have a big enough gas tank to get you to Orlando non-stop.

You put your wife through Hades to get to your vacation spot, and she ends up needing a vacation from going on vacation with you. As a man, you can spend about three days on vacation, and then you are ready to go home because your big picture takes shape. There is no big picture on vacation. You want to go home and get back to work where you produce things. You become mission-minded again; you want to go accomplish something.

Women tend to see the immediate picture before they see the big picture. When it comes to vacation, your wife cares more about the number of pairs of underwear that are packed for you before she cares about getting in the car and going to Orlando. As long as you have a pair on that you can wear into the chlorine-saturated swimming pool for washing each day, then you are okay. She cares if you remembered your toothbrush more than how many miles-per-gallon your car will get and calculating how many stops you'll have to make based on the size of your fuel tank.

You can get a toothbrush at the Walmart in Florida, so to you it doesn't matter if you bring one. If you exclusively planned and prepared for the vacations, the kids wouldn't have anything to wear; they would never eat; and your little girl would still be wearing the same diaper at the end of the vacation. Men just aren't as good at those things. We care about the big picture.

Role #6:
Men have a subconscious desire for companionship.

We are more romantic than women. Neither you

nor your wife would probably agree with that statement, but the romance you displayed in finding a companion outweighed any effort your wife has put forth to be romantic. You chased her, you asked her out, you paid for the dates, you bought the ring, and you planned the honeymoon. Romance declines after the wedding because men achieved their goal. We are goal-oriented. Our goal was to get a companion. We got one, and we feel that we don't have to maintain that effort. We achieved our goal and stopped planning and imagining. Despite our goal orientation, we have a desire for companionship.

Men want companionship so that someone will notice how great they are. What a man likes to hear is his buddy say, "I have to hand it to you, I have never seen anyone do that as well as you." They want recognition from their peer group. Men love the little girl who walks up and says, "You are awesome." A man would do anything to have his girl say that he is awesome. Every man wants his girl to appreciate how incredibly good he is at what he does.

Your wife is the one person whom you want to impress; she is the one whom you want to recognize your greatness. When she says how great you are, you are ready to conquer Hell for her.

Men will go to great lengths for that approval. They

will start a war, go to war, or end a war if their woman will say, "You're my hero." We are pretty simple to figure out. If a woman tells us we are wonderful, then we will jump through the hoops.

You might be a man who has an injured psyche because of mistakes made in the past by you or mistakes that people made in dealing with you. You want the admiration, but you don't trust the words of the person who praises you. Perhaps you have been injured by an abusive home, terrible examples, and loved ones who have betrayed you. You might be skeptical.

You might have a wife who is trying to be your cheerleader, and you are telling her to be quiet because you don't believe what she is saying. What you really believe is that you are a failure, and you feel that people are patronizing you when they say kind words. If you have condemned yourself or lashed out at your wife when she is trying to be your cheerleader, you are displaying the evidence of an unhealed wound; you have judged yourself undeserving of the praise. You married her because you liked her praise, but now you dismiss it. You are caught in a push-pull, and you need counsel because you are stuck between a rock and a hard place.

Men communicate to define who they are. Women communicate to bond with a person. Your wife talks until she feels close. You talk until you have convinced another person that he is on your turf, that it will be done your way, and until you define yourself.

Men talk about how fast their car can go, how fast they can paint the car, how fast they can drive the car, how fast they can fix the car, or how fast they can wash their car; they are just looking for something where they are better than another. Men talk about how big a gun they have and how many birds or deer they have shot. They brag that they shot a 12-point buck, when they didn't even create the deer.

As a man, I am victim to the same things. I have far too many times looked at a little spike-horned buck and pointed my rifle scope at it and thought, "You are not even worth the bullet, you stupid little creature. I deserve you, and you deserve this bullet," and then I pulled the trigger.

I get an ego trip because I shot a deer that has four or five points on each side. Let's face it—we're not that macho! We have guns; deer can only run. If we were really manly, we would use a bow and arrow or run and tackle the deer and stab it with a knife. Hunting isn't what makes us wonderful and important, but such things are how we sometimes judge our manhood. Once we go hunting, we talk about what we did in order to define ourselves.

If you are a man, then you should see yourself in the

roles discussed in this chapter. They are natural to men, so they don't come by choice. This chapter will be the easiest for you to digest because you understand yourself and agree with everything in it. The future chapters will be a challenge because I am going to start defining the roles of your wife, explain how to help your wife fulfill her roles, describe the basic needs of your wife, and challenge you to meet those needs.

CHAPTER TWO

Defining the Role of Your Wife

*J*ust as we did for your role as a husband, I want to show you what the Bible says about your wife's role. I do not want you to misunderstand this chapter. A skeptical person will say that I am down on women. I am not down on women. Ask my wife if I am down on women. Read her books and see if she feels that way. I am very for women, but I am for women being in their role. I am also for men being in their role. I worry that your wife will be discouraged by this chapter. You need to encourage her to read the entire book.

The greatest challenge for a wife is fulfilling her husband's greatest need. The need is described in Ephesians 5. *"Submitting yourselves one to another in the fear of God. Wives, submit yourselves unto your own husbands, as unto the Lord. For the husband is the head of the wife, even as*

Christ is the head of the church: and he is the saviour of the body. Therefore as the church is subject unto Christ, so let the wives be to their own husbands in every thing." (Ephesians 5:21-24)

"Under normal conditions, most people tend to see what they want to see, hear what they want to hear, and do what they want to do; in conflicts, their positions become even more rigid and fixed."

– Marc Robert

The Bible says the husband is the head of the wife. In our society, there are certain areas that we accept a man's being in charge of, but God says that within a marriage he is not just in charge of an area; he is in charge over his wife. The Bible makes that very clear. God appointed your wife to you. A father may say, "I give my blessing to you to marry my daughter," but that father cannot appoint the headship of his son-in-law. God gives a husband that headship.

The ultimate decision that is made in the relationship between a husband and wife is that the wife will decide who runs her. Every other decision and problem will stem from that one decision she will make as a wife. She essentially has to decide if she will or will not submit to God's design. Husband leadership is a great rub in marriage. God's Biblical design is not in accord with many of the excuses that women give for their marital problems. The struggle in marriage is deciding who will be in charge.

The Bible uses the analogy, "*...the husband is the head of the wife, even as Christ is the head of the church.*" When I used to preach around the country, I saw many churches where I felt the people needed to get reconnected to Jesus Christ and figure out that He was in charge of the church. I also saw many churches where if Christ was in charge, then no one knew it. I have seen churches that were run by a mouthy woman. I have seen churches run by a very stubborn, incorrigible man. I have seen churches run by teenagers setting the standards and forcing their parents and adults out of power. I have seen churches that are run by the Super Bowl. I have seen churches that are run by many things other than Jesus Christ, and none of those churches thrive.

The purpose of marriage is to show the world a relationship similar to Christ and His church. That purpose includes your being the head and your wife being submissive to your authority. Why? Because that's what God said.

How do you know if Christ is the head of the church? The Bible tells us in I Corinthians chapters 2 and 3 how we know when Christ is the head of the church. The illustration of headship is the local church because the husband is the head like Christ is the head. The wife is to submit as the church submits to Christ. If we look at that illustration and see the parallels, it should be easy for people to manifest their roles.

"I will therefore that men pray every where, lifting up holy hands, without wrath and doubting. In like manner also, that women adorn themselves in modest apparel, with shamefacedness and sobriety; not with broided hair, or gold, or pearls, or costly array; But (which becometh women professing godliness) with good works. Let the woman learn in silence with all subjection. But I suffer not a woman to teach, nor to usurp authority over the man, but to be in silence." (I Timothy 2:8-12)

The first way to determine if a woman is submissive is if she is not publicly vocal in her disagreements with the church. The Bible says in I Timothy 2 that a church is properly run by the headship of Jesus Christ when men assume the leadership positions. When the Bible says in I Timothy 2:8, *"...men pray every where...,"* it means that men are leading in prayer or leading the church. The passage specifically says that issues of the church need to be addressed by the men and not the women. That idea is repeated later in the passage when it says that women are not to be vocal in the church. The picture in I Timothy is of a church where women are not pushing to have their voice heard.

I have preached in churches where women have approached me and said, "Now let me tell you something. That may work where you come from, but we don't want that kind of preaching here."

I always cut them off and say, "Ma'am, I don't care what you think." I am not very polite to them because the Bible says that this woman's speaking up is a crucial sign that Christ is not the head of the church. I don't work for her; I work for Christ. Nobody is going to insult my Boss. If a man came to me and questioned what I said, I would be glad to discuss it with him. Men have a right to pray or to address or petition the problem.

I am not saying that a woman cannot come to a man of God with a question or problem. When a woman comes to me for a question, I will say, "That is an excellent question. Bring your husband here, and I will answer that question for you." I do that because when a woman disconnects from her husband—whether in the home or in the church—then they have begun the cycle of a lack of subjection. The couple is confusing their roles, and they are going to turn the cart upside down.

When the divorce rate in so-called Bible-believing churches is approximating that of the world, it tells me that something is horrifically wrong in our churches. The one thing that is wrong is we do not have Christ as the head. We have lost the orientation of headship. The influence of a church that is not led by Christ has spread to the marriages within the Christian homes.

Submission is important; it goes back to the book of Genesis. Before the fall of man there is only one reference to Adam's speaking in the first two books of Genesis. It is an indirect reference to Adam's naming the animals. God told Adam to name the animals whatever he chose. The name that Adam chose would be the name of the animal. Whatever Adam said, God agreed on it with him.

The Scriptural importance of submission to a husband's authority is seen in that God demonstrated that what Adam said was what would happen on earth. God agreed with what Adam said. God accepts what a husband says because he is the one in charge. God will hold you accountable for the things unto which your wife submits. If God accepts what you say at face value, then He does not expect your wife to do any less. When a wife is not subject to her own husband, she is defying the example of God and the commands of God.

You might think, "What if I don't believe that?" Matthew 16:15-19 addresses that issue. It says, *"He saith unto them, But whom say ye that I am? And Simon Peter answered and said, Thou art the Christ, the Son of the living God. And Jesus answered and said unto him, Blessed art thou, Simon Barjona: for flesh and blood hath not revealed* *it unto thee, but my Father which is in heaven. And I say also unto thee, That thou art Peter, and upon this rock I will build my church; and the gates of hell shall not prevail against it. And **I will give unto thee** the keys of the kingdom of heaven: and whatsoever **thou** shalt bind on earth shall be bound in heaven: and whatsoever **thou** shalt loose on earth shall be loosed in heaven."*

Jesus was talking to Peter in this passage. Peter was asked if he knew who Jesus was. Peter said that Jesus was "the Christ, the Son of the living God." Peter understood that Jesus was the ultimate authority. Jesus agreed that He had the ultimate authority and then told Peter that He was commissioning authority on earth to Peter. Jesus said that He had decided to accept what Peter wanted to do on earth. If Peter bound it, Jesus bound it. If Peter loosed it, Jesus loosed it.

God says to a wife that she should obey her husband. God does not command her to obey all men, but to obey that one man who is her husband. Ladies should certainly be courteous, polite and kind to other men, but there is only one man they are commanded to obey. Biblical submission is not all women being placed under all men. Biblical submission is one woman following the command to be subject to her one husband.

The Bible uses two military terms, *submit* and *subject*, to describe how a wife should behave toward her husband. These terms are military expressions of rank and file. A wife is to organize herself as to march in rank behind her husband in the cadence that he establishes.

If you say, "Well, then, a wife is nothing but a slave," you are mistaken because the church is not a slave to Christ. Nowhere in the Bible is the church called the slave of Christ, but it is called the bride of Christ. Somebody wisely said, and thousands have repeated, that Eve was not taken from Adam's foot to be walked on, nor was she taken from his head to rule over him. She was taken from his rib to be close to his side and affectionately related to him.

Your wife is not your slave. Military men who go through boot camp do not consider themselves slaves of the military; they consider themselves obedient to the military. There might be a moment in their early days of service when they feel like a slave, but that is not the case. Remember that God chose you to lead your wife. As long as you are alive, you are her superior in command, just like everyone in the military has a superior.

You might be a poor leader, but your wife is still commanded to submit to you. Quality of leadership differs from empowerment of leadership. God empowers you to lead whether you are good at it or not. This book will help you lead your wife, and the companion book will give your wife tips on how to help you lead.

The second way to determine if a woman submits to her husband is through her dress. Smack dab in the middle of I Timothy 2, the Bible is addressing church authority, and it mentions how women dress. The Bible says that you know the church is properly organized and submissive to Christ when the men bring up the issues, the women say nothing, and when the women look like they are in submission to authority.

How your wife dresses should reflect how you would like her to dress. How your wife wears her hair should reflect how you would like her to wear her hair. How does a recruit submit his hairstyle to the Marine Corp? They all have the same haircut because it is a symbol of whom they follow.

The greatest temptation for a woman as she fulfills her role as a wife is to control or change her husband. This happens when a husband won't lead like a wife desires. Your wife is constantly resisting the urge to usurp your authority if you are a bad leader. Problems in your home might come because you have poor leadership skills.

Lack of creativity and lack of thought cause us to have bad marriages. A bad marriage is a lazy marriage. A bad marriage is a marriage where the marriage partners do not want to work and say, "How can I do this?"

When a wife feels that her husband is a poor leader,

she begins to ask herself questions relating to her insecurities. Some of these questions are as follows:

1. Why does God hate me?
2. Why doesn't God love me?
3. How come I feel so left out of my husband's life?
4. Why is my family the only security I have? When they leave me, why do I feel abandoned and left out?

One need that you must fill for your wife is answering these questions. Your wife wants you to lead her because she finds security in that. You might say, "Not my wife; you don't know her." Your wife is a woman, and God made all men and all women with innate desires and feelings. Your wife becomes insecure when she feels that you are not fulfilling your duty of loving as Christ loved the church.

Marriage is not comprised of your being served by your wife. Marriage is a symbiotic relationship where two distinctly different genders each have a role to fulfill for the glorifying of the Lord Jesus Christ. For this organism to thrive, you must do your part to meet the needs of your wife.

CHAPTER THREE

The Needs of Your Wife:

A Stable and Spiritual Leader

*Y*our wife needs a husband who is a stable and spiritual leader. All of your wife's needs are ultimately met by your leadership. Your wife wants you to provide direction. Some of your problems occur because you don't provide direction and leadership, so she figures that she has to provide it. There are basic questions that your wife needs answered.

1. Where are we going in life?
2. Where are you taking me?
3. When are we going to arrive?
4. How are we going to get there?

Seek the Lord. This is the first evidence of a godly Christian leader, and your wife needs one of those in the home. A wife craves to have somebody who can take her closer to God. Eve, the woman, fell into deception in the

Garden of Eden, but she did not realize that she was committing a major sin. Eve thought she was eating fruit that was desired to make one wise; she thought she would get closer to God by partaking of it. She was not yet a sinner, so her desire to be closer to God was not sinful.

Throughout our world, an incredible number of women desire to lead spiritually. The desire is not evil; they are not necessarily trying to best a man. These women are trying to fulfill their desire to be close to God. The desire seems to be stronger for females than it is for males.

"You have to be very careful if you do not know where you're going, because you might not get there."

– Yogi Berra

Adam was a son of God, but he was unique in that God actually made him. Adam did not just talk to God; Adam heard God talk. God placed His own breath in the nostrils of Adam. They had a unique relationship. Eve, in her pre-sinful state, craved to have that. Her first recorded action was a pursuit of God. She wanted someone to lead her to God, even if it was a serpent. She craved to know God.

Perhaps Adam failed to provide leadership, but the bottom line is that we have the same problem today. Women respond better than men do to men of God.

Women respond to the Word of God better than men. Women listen to the teaching of God on the radio more than men. Women watch the preachers on the television more than men. Women are tuned in to God. They buy books and devour spiritual materials. For every book a man *thinks* about reading, a woman will read 25. A woman does so because she is seeking spiritual leadership. Your wife should find that leadership in you.

Your assertion of spiritual leadership is many times more important than any other expression of your manhood. You need to be the one to say that the family is going to church each service. Your ability to swing a bat or a golf club does not impress your wife nearly as much as your having a heart for God.

DIRECTION(S)	
Translation in Wife	*Translation in Husband*
Something her husband must provide spiritually; lack of his provision results in insecurity	Something you will not stop and ask for if you are lost

Your wife needs to know that you delight in the Lord and that you are getting your direction from Him. Direction comes from a consistent and growing relationship with the Lord. The following is a list of some evidences that your life shows a desire to seek the Lord:

- A regular time in God's Word
- Consistent memorization of Scriptures
- Faithfulness in prayer
- Regular church attendance
- Fellowship with the right kinds of sincere and godly Christians
- Discussion of spiritual matters

Do these evidences express your desire and characterize your life? How would your wife answer these questions about your walk with God? Do you have a stash of Christian books that you read, or do you have a stash of pornography? Do you keep journals about your Bible reading? You are made in the image of God; are there any similarities to Him? Do your friends crave God, or do they talk about only jobs, money, and sex? Your talk tells a lot about your heart and how much you seek the Lord.

CONVICTION(S)	
Translation in Wife	Translation in Husband
What her husband should exhibit as he applies Biblical standards to their lives	What his wife should do because he knows he is right and she should trust him

Have convictions based on the Scriptures. As your

wife sees you establishing God's standards in your life, she will be motivated to submit to your leadership and set similar standards in her own life. The first evidence of Scriptural convictions is the demonstration of your love for God by loving your wife, children, and others. A renewed love for your wife will do wonders for her stability.

The second evidence of Scriptural convictions is avoiding actions or activities that might cause your wife or children or others to stumble. Many a wife has told me that her husband turns on a DVD or the television and lets their children see things they shouldn't see. How many underwear ads have you allowed your children to see because they were advertisements during your favorite show? How many macho male shows do you justify watching even though they contain

"It's not hard to make decisions when you know what your values are."

– Roy Disney

explicit sexual scenes and then market lingerie during the commercial breaks?

The macho hero of prime-time programming may fire a gun and be a modern-day superman, but he is damning your spiritual leadership. Masculinity does not have to include immorality. Nothing is macho about the striptease shows that are aired on television. Decide to make your home a center of godly learning and godly living.

Develop a determination to follow convictions. Consistent obedience to the convictions you profess to believe provide the strength and example your wife needs to obey God and you. She will find stability when she sees you following God.

What is the obstacles that is hindering you from consistently obeying God's Word and following His standards? If you are like most men, it is the influence of television. If you are like most men, it is the influence of the wrong friends.

Don't defend your friend's misdeeds. He might be your buddy, but you don't need to go on a hunting trip with him if he is a boozer, has a pornography addiction, or has a filthy marriage. If he has a poor marriage, he probably isn't a good influence on your marriage. I have counseled marital problems over a husband's not giving up a friend who swatted his wife's rear end and lusted after her. The husband was influenced by his friend to talk about sexy women and sexy jokes, while the wife wondered where his convictions were. This is a typical problem.

Other obstacles to following convictions are losing your temper and maintaining the wrong priorities. Men don't make church a priority and show a temper that is un-Christian. The wife watches and finds no stability in her saved but backslidden husband.

Do not let past sins and failures be an obstacle to your being a stable and spiritual leader. You are a man, and manly leadership says, "I go forward." Manly leadership does not say, "I have slept with women, and I love pornography, so I can't cope with being a husband."

"The means by which we live have outdistanced the ends for which we live. Our scientific power has outrun our spiritual power. We have guided missiles and misguided men."

– Martin Luther King, Jr.

Men love heroes in action programs and great sports comebacks because men love to rise to the occasion. They love when someone triumphs against all odds. They love that except when it is in their marriage. If you love action shows and sports, why don't you triumph against all odds in your marriage? When you think that you can't cope, why don't you rise to the occasion like your imaginary hero would?

Your sports and movie heroes are simply examples— real or imaginary—of men who are doing what you refuse to do. Overcome your baggage and realize that a wife and kids need you to save them. Picture them as weaker people who need a strong man to rise to the occasion. Your family needs you to rise out of the morbidity of your failures and say, "I've made mistakes, but I'm going forward."

Don't be in bondage to enslaving habits, pride, and willful sinning. I do not understand the modern man who says, "That is just the way I am," when he is confronted with his sin. Your wife thought that she married a stronger man with strong convictions. A man should look at his wife and say, "I'm sorry. It was wrong, and it will never happen again as long as there is a Heaven and a Hell." Your heart needs to be sold out to God, and it does not need to prove that it has a right to do whatever it wants.

Display love no matter what happens. The evidence of being led and motivated by God's Spirit is having the fruit of the Spirit in all your actions. The number-one evidence of the fruit of the Spirit is love. Could you list five ways in which you display your love to your wife? You need to and should because you need to take an honest look at whether or not your wife feels her need for love is being fulfilled.

For the sake of your wife, develop some spirituality. She yearns to have stability with the matters concerning her God. Love your wife at all times because you are her example of God in the home. She is looking for spiritual leadership, and she wants you to provide it.

CHAPTER FOUR

The Needs of Your Wife:

Knowing That She Is Meeting Vital Needs in Your Life That No Other Woman Can Meet

*Y*our wife must feel that she is uniquely special to you. Telling her that she is special is insufficient; she wants to know how she is special. God made her to be a helper who is suitable and appropriate for you. The needs that a wife is meeting must be of importance to her husband because the more important the needs are to him, the more he will praise and appreciate her.

The most devastating action of a husband is to assign one of his wife's special tasks to another woman. An even worse move is made when the husband praises the other woman for doing it. The scourge of a woman is jealousy. Jealousy is the fear of being displaced.

Women become jealous because they feel that whatever role they have in fulfilling or satisfying the needs of a man is being replaced or displaced by some other woman. Your wife doesn't want your needs met by a woman at work, a woman at church, a woman on the bus route, a woman down the hallway, a neighbor woman, your daughter, your relative, your sister, or your mother. You wife wants you to be her kingdom, and she wants to take care of all of your needs. A wife will never get over another woman's taking over her role.

"THAT LADY WAS A BIG HELP TO ME."	
Translation in Wife	*Translation in Husband*
1. She is replacing me. 2. My husband doesn't need me anymore.	That lady was a help to me.

Recognizing the potential for this problem is especially important in the workplace. A man must choose his female staff very carefully. American society now has men and women working together. This has introduced problems of which Christian men must make themselves aware.

I have had women working with me for 25 years, and I have implemented certain policies and procedures to make sure that there was a wall that would keep me from becoming too close to them and allowing them to take the place of my wife. When I hired a woman, I followed these policies.

POLICY #1:
Never hire a lady you think is looking for you to meet her emotional needs.

From the beginning, I explain to the people who work with me that we have a professional system even though I am also their pastor. We always establish when a lady is coming to me as her pastor or as her employer. If she comes to me because she needs a pastor, then I suggest that she bring her husband when we meet. Certainly a woman is allowed to talk to me initially as her pastor, but ultimately I deal with a woman's problems by talking to the husband and wife.

As a boss, I am not the one who should be giving emotional encouragement or strength to my lady employees. I am supposed to give that encouragement and strength to my wife. Attempting to meet the emotional needs of women in the workplace is certain to produce insecurity in your wife and will likely produce jealousy and resentment.

A lady's basic emotional needs must be met by her parents if she is single, by her husband if she is married, and by God if she is widowed.

POLICY #2:

Allow your wife to approve the ladies who work closely with you.

My wife has approved every lady who works in my office. Technically, a secretary is working for your wife since she is doing things to assist you that your wife is not able to do at the workplace. If you gave your wife veto power over hiring staff ladies, you would be making a big statement to her. When I hire a lady, she is working for my wife; the secretary is not an extension of me. Before I consider a woman, I ask my wife to give me a list of ladies who meet her approval. I then interview from that list.

POLICY #3:

Keep your relationship with your secretaries or females in the office on a business level at all times.

Do not become involved in their personal lives. When they have serious problems, they need to go to a husband or pastor. You are not there to provide that personal help. Build an absolute brick wall between the two and say, "Sorry, I can't help you with that. I hired you to answer the phone, or I hired you to type letters, and I really need to keep our relationship to those professional areas. I just won't cross that line with you."

POLICY #4:

Make sure your wife can call you directly without going through any females in your office.

Cell phones are good for this. Your wife should never have to feel that she has to be put on hold to get you. I have a policy that I answer a call from my wife regardless of with whom I am meeting. My wife always has access to me, and you should make a way for your wife to always have access to you.

POLICY #5:

Never ask staff ladies to meet personal needs or perform special tasks that your wife normally does.

When you begin to have your female staff run your errands, you are starting to replace your wife. The ladies on your staff should have specific duties, and out of concern for your wife, you should not have them stray from those duties.

POLICY #6:

Praise your wife to the ladies in your office and never discuss marriage with them.

I have never said to a lady in my office, "I am having a marital struggle." There have been days when my wife and I have had struggles, but I don't go to the office and voice them. Neither do I want the ladies in my office coming to my office and telling me their problems because I want them to retain the integrity of their marriages.

Your office staff should be committed to the success of your marriage, and you should be committed to the success of their marriages. Our marriages supersede our jobs and ministries. No matter how urgent a ministry becomes, it can never take the place of the urgency of your marriage.

If you work in an arena where your wife is not welcome, then you have to take greater precautions that a woman doesn't have access to you that your wife doesn't have. You need to call your wife periodically throughout the day. Remind her of what you are doing and that you are thinking about her and that she is important to you.

A common problem in marriages is that a man never gives his wife a role that is uniquely hers. This problem does not just apply to the realm of a man's job, but it applies at home, too. Men have artificial women on a computer screen that give them sexual satisfaction. Men have secretaries to get them coffee, a newspaper, breakfast, and lunch. Men have secretaries that furnish the needs of his staff. They have secretaries who clean, cook, run errands, and buy gifts. If that is the case, then what does the wife do for that husband?

This is why men have mental affairs where they fantasize in their heart about another woman. This is why men have physical affairs with the women amongst whom they work. This is why men have spiritual affairs where they displace their wife under the guise of work, or business, or serving the Lord. Are you at fault in any of these? If so, you are telling your wife that there is nothing in your life that she is capable of fulfilling or necessary to accomplish. You are basically saying, "I don't need you."

When a man won't make time for his wife, then he is saying, "Even if I had a need, I don't need you to fill it." The tendency for a man is not to share his real needs with his wife. You want your wife to admire your success, but your success won't win her love. You will win her love more by sharing your specific failures than by reporting your successes. Your wife is not as impressed with your ability to succeed as she is with what you need and how she can help.

Even I want everyone else in the world to think that I am self-confident, self-capable, and self-supplied. I want people to think that they need me more than I need them. Every man thinks this way. A wife wants to know that if you are a success, that she helped you to arrive at that destination. She wants to help you stay on that pinnacle and to know that she helps keep you there.

If you work for someone, you love when they need you to come through. You don't want to be useless at your job. You love it when the boss says, "Can you do me a favor? I need you to drop what you are doing and come into my office. I am in a pickle and need you to help." You love that because you want to rise to the occasion. You know that you can come through for him. Multiply that feeling by ten, and you will understand how much your wife wants to help you. What need is your wife meeting that no other woman can meet? The following are some needs that the Bible says only she can meet.

• **Your wife gives you the potential to have power in your prayer life.** She is the basis of your most important message, the illustration of how Christ loves the church. I Peter 3:7 says, *"Likewise, ye husbands, dwell with them according to knowledge, giving honour unto the wife, as unto the weaker vessel, and as being heirs together of the grace of life; that your prayers be not hindered."* The union that you have with your wife illustrates the oneness that you have with Christ. God looks at how close you and He are on the issue of unity when you pray. God looks at the emotional and spiritual union that you have with your wife. He answers your prayers relative to the unity you have with Him, which is displayed through your relationship with your wife. Men whose relationship with their wife is not right don't pray because they know that it wouldn't do any good.

• **Your wife is an alarm system against other women with wrong motives.** If you can't stand your wife yapping about other women, you need to realize that she is protecting you and warning you. Your wife is jealous for you. You should be glad for that because she protects you morally.

• **Your wife is a safeguard to your hasty decisions because of her need for security and consistency.** Your wife is like a flywheel. She keeps you from over revving. She keeps you from doing stupid things because she expresses fears that you don't understand. Your wife can keep you from quitting something; she gets you to think it over. A wife slows her husband down from getting into or out of things.

• **Your wife is the one woman who can give you the joy of a physical relationship without guilt.** No matter how intense or wild sex is with your wife, you never feel a twinge of guilt after having sex with her unless you can't get over past guilt of immoral sexual relations. Guys who are hung up on pornography can't stand themselves after they gratify themselves because they have no masculine stability. The lack of control causes them to feel like less of a man. A man doesn't feel that way when he is with his wife. Your wife can give you guilt-free sex; take advantage of that.

- **Your wife instills godly attitudes in children.** She is the one that teaches them that father always knows best. She is the one who teaches them that Daddy is the smartest man in the world. Your wife is the one who will discern the real needs of your children when you are too preoccupied with your job. She spends more time with them than you do, so she can be more of an influence for righteousness.

Once upon a time you couldn't wait to see your wife and be around her because she brought happiness with her presence. There was a time that she brought you joy that nothing else could. Where did that go? Did she change, or did you change? Have you stopped giving your wife the opportunities to meet your needs? As her husband, you should find duties for your wife and allow only her to complete them. The joy she feels will ease some of her anxiety and envy.

CHAPTER FIVE

The Needs of Your Wife:

Seeing That You Cherish Her and That You Delight in Her as a Person

*T*he key word in the chapter title is *cherish*. During a wedding ceremony, men vow to cherish their wife, but few men know what that beautiful and well-scripted word means.

Neither do men know how to cherish their wives. The word *cherish*, when pertaining to your wife, has three meanings:

1. To see great value in her as a person
2. To protect her
3. To praise her to others

If you cherish your wife, then you value what she is as a human being. Your wife needs to know she is a vital part of your world. Too often wives are accessories and not vital organs of their husbands' world. It is essentially important for your wife to know that your delight in her goes beyond the things that she can do for you. Is your wife of any value to you other than the person who cooks and cleans up your home?

The typical husband would say that his wife is:

1. A cook
2. A housekeeper
3. A sex partner
4. The person who rears his children

You could hire someone to perform all of those duties. What does your wife uniquely provide for you? That's a question you need to answer.

The problem with many husbands is that they do not value the personhood of their wife. A husband tends to value what his wife can do for him. Unfortunately, most of what a man would list as something he needs from his wife could be fulfilled by any woman.

You have marriage struggles because your wife knows that she is easily displaced. You wife needs to hear you talk about the character qualities, the personality traits, and the family qualities that attracted you to her. She needs to hear you talk about the evidences of God's leading that brought the two of you together. If you have a typical marriage, then your wife never hears those things.

When I perform marriages, I tell the story of how the

man first noticed the woman. Sadly, that is often the last time a woman hears about how attractive she was to her husband. Unfortunately, it came from my lips instead of his. You should relive those wonderful moments with your wife.

You wife loves when you talk of her qualities that you find attractive. Your wife desires evidence that convinces her that what once made her important from all other women is still important today. Men miss out on cherishing their wife because they neglect communicating the historical perspective.

Throughout the Bible God repeats the telling of His greatest accomplishments. Many times God repeats the law. Many times the story of the Red Sea's parting is recalled. God repeats Himself because He is trying to form a relationship with the reader. In its simplest form, the Bible starts off with God by Himself and ends with the Spirit and the bride going off into an eternal sunset. The Bible is a love story; it is filled with the retelling of many stories.

Your wife wants that in your marriage. She wants to know if there is any connection between what you have now and what you had then. She wants you to tell her one more time how it all came to be. When was the last time you rehearsed how you and your wife met? When was the last time you told her what captivated you?

The growing proof that you cherish your wife is your ability to take unchangeable past experiences (molestation, abuse, mishandling by a parent or authority, physical features or defects) and turn them into praiseworthy attributes. Your wife might have an emotional tic where she flinches at certain things, but you have to help her view those issues from God's perspective. When she gains that perspective, she will develop an inner radiance and a significant light. You cherish your wife when you work to help her instead of wondering what is wrong with her.

"Treat people as if they were what they ought to be and you help them to become what they are capable of being."

– Johann Wolfgang von Goethe

Fixing the past hurts of your wife is your responsibility. Your challenge is to transform her view of the unchangeable flaws from insurmountable to providential. Your challenge is to take the flaws and turn them into greatness that she can easily recognize.

Telling your wife to get over something is the ignorantly easy way to handle a situation. However, it is even easier to become cruel because you forget that your wife doesn't think like you, nor is she built like you. She is not a female version of you. Your wife is wired differently than you. You are an IBM, and she is a Macintosh. You are both computers, but you have different software, different microprocessors, and different operating systems.

"Everyone is kneaded out of the same dough but not baked in the same oven."

– Yiddish Proverb

Cherishing requires that you take your wife's failures, hurts, and heartaches of the past; accept them; and give her God's perspective on those matters. If you are going to give her God's perspective, then you need to have a good understanding of God's sovereignty. You need to be able to articulate that into your wife's life. Your wife needs to see that the flaws which intimidate and humiliate her are the attributes that make her unique and wonderful to you. As a husband, you should be saying:

1. "I like you because of that."
2. "I enjoy that unique part of you."
3. "I am thrilled with the challenge that your difficulties represent to me."
4. "I love that we can discuss these matters."

Saying these things is hard for a husband because they interfere with his television watching and hobbies designed to ignore his wife. She probably sits around as a lonely woman who is wondering if she is loved because she sees her hurts as unlovable. It is your job to cherish her and delight in her personhood. Your wife is consumed with what you think about her. If she knew that she was cherished, she would feel a security that enables her to cope with her deficiencies.

CHAPTER SIX

The Needs of Your Wife:

Knowing That You Understand Her by Protecting Her in the Areas of Her Limitations

*E*very wife has a deep need to be understood. The Bible says in I Peter 3:7, *"Likewise, ye husbands, dwell with them according to knowledge…."* A husband needs to know his wife. God commands you to know and understand your wife. Most men think they understand their wives, but most men are mistaken.

"Be not disturbed at being misunderstood; be disturbed at not understanding."

– Chinese Proverb

A most basic misunderstanding is found in boundaries. Many husbands build the wrong type of boundaries that neglect their wife. She might push you until she finds out where her boundaries are. Boundaries of love are very important because, by definition, love has boundaries. No boundaries equates to no love.

What would sports be without boundaries? What if there were no sidelines in football? The game would be dumb if a player could just run behind the bench or up into the stands on the way to the end zone. Boundaries allow people to participate and to enjoy the game.

Your wife wants boundaries that show a concern for her. Your wife wants you to be aware of her spiritual, mental, emotional, and physical strengths and weaknesses. She wants you to have the wisdom and courage to provide loving yet firm direction so she will not fail by going beyond her limitations.

Occasionally your wife will ask you for something she does not really want. She is testing to see if you are perceptive to her real needs and dangers. If you give her whatever she wants, she will become insecure. This is exactly what happened in the Garden of Eden. Failure in a marriage is often catalyzed by a man's always believing that his wife means, "I want that." A common mistake for a husband is working to give his wife everything she wants. This goes back to the premise of the book. Your wife is saying something in her Wife language. You cannot take those words for face value in your Husband language.

When your wife says, "I think I should work," she may not mean that; remember that she is speaking Wife. She is searching for the boundaries that you are establishing in your marriage. If she says, "I'll take over the finances if you would like," she doesn't necessarily want to do that. She is asking you, "Where are the

"The most important thing in communication is to hear what isn't being said."

– Peter F. Drucker

boundaries you have given me?" She doesn't say it so succinctly because no wife likes to have her limitations defined. Your wife is trying to feel out her limitations.

Your wife needs to know if you can properly translate her language. Your wife wants to know if you are wise enough to discern and say, "Sweetheart, let's talk about that. I am not sure that is a real good idea. Let's talk about your strengths and weaknesses, what you need, and what you don't need." The conversation would do more for your wife than getting or not getting that for which she asked.

"People who are only good with hammers see every problem as a nail."

– Abraham Maslow

You must know your wife so well that you understand when

to be firm and when to be lenient. Loving firmness will be respected when you both know in your spirit that the firmness is appropriate. Your wife is very susceptible to men who understand her. She is frustrated with any man who does not understand her, especially those who say they do, but do not.

A woman is turned off when someone thinks that he does understand, but she knows that he doesn't. The biggest turn on to a woman is a man who understands her. I tell every counselor that the most dangerous position you are in is when a woman you are counseling says, "I am so glad you understand me." That's a warning sign that you should stay away from that woman.

A husband needs to learn how to discern his wife's needs. He needs to understand when she really needs something. Your wife wants to know that you understand her needs and that you will protect her from entering areas where she is vulnerable.

CHAPTER SEVEN

The Needs of Your Wife:

Knowing That You Enjoy Setting Aside Time for Intimate Conversation With Her

*I*ntimate conversation is a basic need of your wife, but she also wants to know that you enjoy it. Intimate conversation is only possible when there is a unity of spirit. Couples who live with a conflict of spirit never have intimate conversation. When you come home each day, your wife has more things to talk about than you probably suspect. Men are often talked out when they arrive home while women have a ton to talk about when they arrive home. Bridging that gap is essential for your wife.

A wife can spend two hours talking about a twenty-minute phone call that she enjoyed with a friend or with her mother. The wise husband will want to hear every detail and ask questions about it. Your wife enjoys sharing these important things only if she knows that you enjoy listening and are not eager to do something else. When you twirl your keys as she is talking to you, she correctly figures that you just don't care. She has you pegged when you can't turn off the television as she is speaking to you; she knows that you aren't really interested in her. If your wife senses that you are preoccupied or in a hurry, she will not talk unless she is desperate, and then she will probably yell.

"You cannot truly listen to anyone and do anything else at the same time."

– M. Scott Peck

Your wife is willing to make a sacrifice of not having deep, intimate conversation about the things that are truly important to her if you have really, truly important things that must be done. You cannot abuse that loyalty from your wife. However, she will sour on your marriage when you don't have time to talk to her, but you have time to talk on the phone to people about trivial matters or to surf the Internet.

The key to intimate conversation is having a regular time planned for it. Half of your wife's enjoyment in talking is anticipating the time you are going to get together and talk. A wife enjoys knowing it is coming.

If your wife wrote you a sexually suggestive note and

told how she was going to please you when you got home, then you would count down the time until you got home from work. You would find a way to get out of work early. You would do your full day of work in two hours and hope that the boss would let you off early for a job well done.

Your wife has similar anticipation for the times the two of you can talk. Men have a hard time believing that because they cannot compute how sex and talking could compare. However, your wife thrives on talking. Your intimacy preference is physical; her intimacy preference is verbal.

Here are several questions you need to answer as a husband:

1. When is the regular time that you and your wife have intimate conversation to discuss the things that matter deeply to her?

2. Where are the places that your wife enjoys going in order to have that intimate conversation? Is it over breakfast at her favorite restaurant? Is it walking through a certain park or trail? Where does she really open up to you?

3. What things do you enjoy sharing with your wife? What is it that you cannot wait to share with your wife?

4. Who is the person with whom you can't wait to

share something? The answer to that question is the person who is important in your life. Do you ever get excited about telling your wife anything?

There was a time that you were excited about talking to your wife; that is how you attracted her. What was it that you couldn't wait to talk about on the phone? How was it that you talked for hours on end? You could talk for hours about nothing because she was the sweet angel of your fantasies, but now she is no longer that desire because you have more important things to do.

Wives have deep fears and emotions. It is likely that they have never shared these with their husbands. A wife will not share these feelings with her husband for the following reasons:

- She feels guilty for having them.
- She hopes they will pass.
- She fears rejection from her husband.
- She desires to reduce her husband's burdens.
- She knows you don't have the answers.

Your wife already knows how you respond to her fears. Your wife finds out how you respond to her fears and whether or not you have answers by telling you about another woman who has similar problems. She then watches to see if you have compassion, understanding, patience and practical help, or if you blow it off and say, "Why don't they get a life." You are telling your wife how you will respond if she has the same problem.

The fears of your wife are a test of your love because the Bible says in I John 4:18, *"...perfect love casteth out fear...."* This verse does not mean that when your wife loves you perfectly, she will then be released from her fears. When your wife receives your perfect love, it casts away her fears. The passage is speaking about how God loves us, and His love removes our fears. The spiritual parallel teaches that when I love my wife, my love removes her fears.

A husband has to understand the challenge a wife sees in her emotional and spiritual weaknesses and strengths. She wonders if her husband is going to receive them with a patient understanding. She tests you by talking about her friends. Some of them exist and some of them don't. Sometimes she tells you about a problem her friend is having because she wants to know how you would treat her in that situation. Sometimes she makes friends up so that she can see how you will react.

When your wife says, "I was talking to Laura," you need to tune in to what she is saying. You need to ask her questions about her conversation with "Laura." You should ask your wife, "What else did Laura say?" You should not ask your wife, "Did this really happen?" Don't let her know that you might be on to her feelers.

Cats use their whiskers to help them decide if they

can fit into a crevice. Your wife is doing the same thing when she talks about her friends. She is feeling out whether she can fit into the cradle of your security.

Security is what will give your wife the confidence to say, "Can I tell you something that I have never told anyone else before?" You have to encourage your wife and coax her into revealing her heart. I love long, deep conversations with my wife. I love it when she says, "I can't believe that I tell you all these things that are inside of me." I can believe that she tells me these things because I am the man that has proven that I can be trusted with her heart. Sadly, most husbands fail at proving that they are worthy of their wife's heart.

Start by having a regular time and some regular places where the two of you talk. Looking forward to a time is half of the enjoyment for your wife. Be steadfast in keeping that time because it is precious to her. Develop a relationship of communication. You will find that you enjoy it, and your wife will find joy in knowing that you enjoy those times together.

CHAPTER EIGHT

The Needs of Your Wife:

Knowing That You Are Aware of Her Presence Even When You Are Not With Her

A wife needs to know that her husband is thinking about her at all times. Your awareness of your wife's presence is assurance to her of your love and protection. My father-in-law taught me this when I dated my wife. He would say, "If you can convince your girlfriend that you want to be with her when you are not with her, you will own her heart." He would talk to the young men at Hyles-Anderson College and say, "If you want to get married, convince her that you can't go on without her even when you are not with her."

Your job is to manipulate your schedule in such a way that she thinks you are thinking about her all the time even when you are not with her. Your job is not to convince her that you are busy, a hotshot, or have a lot of responsibility. Your job is for her to think that all you do is think about her. Your wife should think that you talk about her at work. Do not tell your wife, "I am so busy at work that I don't know what I think any more," because she will know that you are not thinking about her.

Sometimes a wife is so desperate to know whether you think about her that she will flat out ask you. If your wife asks you that question, then you have not successfully convinced her that you think about her. A wife recalls with vivid detail how aware of her you were when you first met her. She feels shut out and lonely if you are no longer aware of her.

Remember when you were dating? You sat on the phone and talked for hours about nothing. When was the last time you talked on the phone about nothing with your wife? When I pose that question to men during counseling, the typical response is, "I only have so many cell phone minutes." Wow! That is romantic.

When I deal with a man who has had an affair, I usually find that he spends 1,700 to 3,000 minutes per month talking to his fling. The wife would be ecstatic to have her husband talk to her half of that time. When I ask the man what he and his mistress talked about, he usually responds, "Nothing." Three thousand minutes of nothing? He used to do that with his wife, and she would love it if they could do that again.

How are you doing at making your wife feel remembered? Is it "business-as-usual" since you got married? Do you make efficient phone calls to her? Efficiency is not the goal in marriage. Waste, indulgence, and blowing money for no reason at all—that is what marriage is about.

Taking care of your wife's needs is one way that you express that you are aware of her presence. My bank account contained $12,000 when I got married, and I have been in debt ever since. I am going to tell you how I have financed my marriage. No financial advisor would ever tell you to do this, but I am telling my story as the pastor of a large church who is happily married and has two children who are married and work in the ministries at my church.

Throughout the years that I have worked in the ministry, I have not made a great salary—God has always provided, but it has not been a salary that gets a man ahead in life. I have financed my marriage by refinancing my house. Every time the interest rate dropped one and one-half percent, I refinanced the mortgage, added $10,000 of equity to the loan, and used the money to pay off my credit card debts.

Since I had a wife and two small children, I didn't want to get a second job that would take me away from them and make me counterproductive as a family man.

My second job was watching the interest rates come down so I could refinance again. After 25 years of marriage, I owed the same amount of money on my house that I did when I purchased it. That's not great worldly financial wisdom, but it is wisdom on how to handle your finances while rearing kids and providing for your wife on a tight budget. Now that I have reared my children and they are married, I will pay off a seven-year note on my house before I am 55 years old.

The secret is to get a good house that has equity in it, buy low, and keep refinancing. A house is a money pump. You make about three-to-seven percent every year on a house. If you don't mind owing a lot of money when your kids get married, it is a great plan. Once the kids are married, you will have a lot more money to pay off the house. Of course you have to know how much you can handle before you drown. But you have to do something in order to afford your marriage and make your wife feel secure.

You can live on your love, but that will probably lead to a lot of fighting. It costs money to be happy. If you are shocked by that statement, then welcome to America! You don't have to be splurging and indulgent, but it helps to be so now and then. You need to spend the money that is necessary to make your wife feel that you are thinking of her.

Manners are an important way in which you show your wife that you are aware of her presence. Why do women want manners in a man? Women equate manners with attentiveness to someone's presence. Men often wonder how women remember so much, but it is simply because they are tuned in to their surroundings. If I go to a restaurant five times, I could tell you if they have good food. My wife could tell you the color of the walls, the outfit that the waitress wears, and how the bathroom is decorated.

Women are tuned in to their surroundings. When you are tuned in to your wife, she is very tuned in to the fact that you are tuned in to her. A husband that displays manners is telling his wife that he is tuned in to her presence. A husband that displays manners is telling those around him that he thinks a lot about his wife. Manners make your wife feel loved, and it is such an easy way to say I love you.

Manners that a husband should display are ordering for his wife at a restaurant, opening the car door for her, helping her take off her coat, seating her at a table, opening entryway doors for her, lifting heavy objects, and replacing light bulbs. Your wife thinks it is awesome when you display manners. None of these are goofy, weird, or queer. They are not related to education or being well bred. Manners are a display of maturity and love for your wife. When she sees a man who has better manners than you, she wonders why you don't love her as much as another man loves his wife. Manners aren't feminine; manners display that you care.

You need to develop the manner of properly introducing your wife. She must always be mentioned first because you always first introduce the person of greater rank, authority, or prestige. If she met your boss, you would say, "Sweetheart, I want you to meet my boss." You should not say, "Boss, I want you to meet my wife," because he is not more important than your wife. Manners magnify your wife. You make a statement to everyone around that she is the highest person of stature in your life.

Proper manners include being punctual, telling her your schedule, and allowing her direct access to your work phone without having to go through anybody else in your office. Proper manners include refraining from crude language, criticism, and improper subjects. Proper manners include personal cleanliness, neatness, and grooming.

If you are weak in any of those areas, it is perfectly acceptable to say to your wife, "I didn't have the kind of training that I think you deserve in a man. I would like you to help me." Your wife will not think that you are weak. A wife will take great humble joy in teaching you;

she won't be angry or upset. She will be excited that you want to learn these things. A wife always thinks she is serving you when you ask her for advice or training; she never thinks she is superior to you. What she hates is your arrogant and incorrect assumptions that lead to embarrassment.

Husbands need to develop manners for listening to their wife. When a wife asks her husband a question, he should:

"Listening, not imitation, may be the sincerest form of flattery."

1. Stop what he is doing.
2. Look at her.
3. Smile when she talks.
4. Answer her questions, even the little ones.

– Dr. Joyce Brothers

5. Tell her with his eyes that he loves her.

There is an art to answering questions. Don't keep looking at the paper or television when she asks you a question. Impress your wife by putting the paper down or turning down the television when she asks you a question. When you don't give her your undivided attention, she knows that you are not even considering her presence.

When your wife asks where you are going to eat on your date night, don't say, "I don't know. What do you think?" You need to put down the newspaper and say, "I am afraid I got busy today, and I didn't even think about supper tonight. I would like to go to a fun restaurant. Where would you like to go? You choose three and I pick, or I choose three and you pick." Make a game of the date night, but at least show her that you are giving her some thought.

"Could a greater miracle take place than for us to look through each other's eyes for an instant?"

– Henry David Thoreau

When your wife asks which of you is picking up the kids from an activity, you should put down the paper, push the mute button, look her right in the eyes, and say, "I thought if we made passionate love, I would probably go pick them up. What do you think?"

A wife needs to know that her husband is not just talking to the stranger next door, but that he is talking to the one person in the whole world that matters most to him. A husband needs to let his wife know that he is not talking to his wife like he would talk to his boss or other employees. A wife needs to know that she is special to her husband.

You do enjoy your wife's presence, don't you? Remind your wife that you enjoy her presence. Convince your wife that you enjoy her presence. She might overlook the little things that lead to disagreements if she knows you like being with her because those little things pale in comparison to knowing that she has your heart and mind.

Chapter Nine

The Needs of Your Wife:

Seeing That You Are Making Investments in Her Life That Will Fulfill Her World

The first investment that you need to make in your wife's life is a spiritual investment. Most husbands don't think about the spiritual development of their wife. However, as her protector, you must protect her spirit as well as her physical body. If you are going to invest in her spirit, then you need to learn her spiritual gifts. Here are questions that you should answer in order to discern how you can help your wife:

1. What are your wife's strengths?
2. Does your wife need to work in the nursery because she has a gift for that?
3. Does she need to have a part-time job someplace in a ministry because she has valuable skills and gifts?

4. Does she need to be a volunteer in more areas of the church because it is healthy for her?

I am afraid that most men make decisions because their wife will stop pestering them once they make the decision the way she wants. That is weak leadership. A husband who is strong and leads will learn to discern his wife's strengths and weaknesses. If you allow your wife to pursue an area where she is not spiritually gifted, then your marriage and church might be grieved.

Your wife needs you to define *her* responsibilities in the home. Your wife also needs you to define *your* responsibilities in the home. A husband who does not invest in his wife by simply defining responsibilities creates frustration for his wife. When roles are undefined, a wife will feel overwhelmed with the responsibility of running the entire home and resent her husband who treats his home like a bed and breakfast. You and your wife need to sit down and list the duties that need to be done and assign who in the family (including the children) is responsible for each duty.

It might be wise to assign a day of the week to a specific duty. Monday could be laundry day, and everybody is assigned a laundry duty. Someone sorts, someone fills up the washer, someone is responsible for transferring the clothes to the dryer, someone is responsible for folding the clothes, and someone is responsible for putting away the clothes. Tuesday could be shopping day, and Wednesday could be cleaning day. A husband and wife need to sit down and define what types of groceries will be purchased so that a wife who shops knows what is expected of her. Your wife wants to please you and take care of your home. You might be unfair when you criticize her choices of food and timeliness of cleaning when you have never expressed to her how you would like those chores to be accomplished. A variety of chores need to be done, and you and your wife need to sit down and figure out when each one will be done.

When my wife and I were engaged and preparing for marriage, she said, "Tell me what things you like to eat."

I honestly replied, "I have never met a food I didn't like, but I have met some that I didn't want to meet again. I will eat anything you put in front of me, but I have preferences."

Curious, she replied, "What are some things you prefer not to have?"

I gladly told her, "I love the taste of liver, but I just can't get over what it does in the body. It is a filter. Eating liver is like eating the air filter in the furnace. I have a hard time eating a dirty part of an animal. I don't like eating liver."

My wife replied, "Oh, I love liver."

I said, "You cook it, and I will eat it."

So she cooked it many times, and I ate it. She asked me, "Are you enjoying this?"

I said, "Sure I am enjoying this; I am with you."

She replied, "No, I don't mean do you enjoy being with me. I mean do you enjoy the liver?"

I said, "I love being with you. I thoroughly enjoy it. Time spent with you is always good regardless of what we are doing."

She said, "You don't like liver."

I said, "The taste is impeccable. The taste of liver is very good. It stinks, but other than that it tastes good."

She said, "But you don't enjoy it."

I said, "I told you before—I have never met a food I didn't like, but if we never had it again, I wouldn't cry." She hasn't prepared liver for me in years, but when I am out of town, my wife splurges and eats liver and Brussels sprouts.

Discussing duties at your house is as exciting as watching mud harden, but the bottom line is that you must talk with your wife about the things where she lives. I understand that she lives with a lot of duties that you don't enjoy, but you must make the investment of defining those duties to fulfill needs in her world.

You probably don't understand what it takes to shop for food. It is a pain in the neck to shop for a family. As a man, you never want to go to a supermarket, but she has to so that you can eat. First of all, she has to buy everything on the budget you give her. If you are like most men, you don't give your wife enough money to buy food. As kids grow older, one becomes fussy about certain foods, and another becomes fussy about certain brands. You get fussy about the style of potato chips, and she needs to buy whole milk and skim milk to make everyone happy. After a while the complaining will get to your wife. She wants to get what you like, but eventually she is going to say, "Well, that's what we have to eat, so deal with it." You will start thinking that your wife can't run the house, and you won't like the way she is doing anything. Ultimately, you are at fault because you have not helped your wife organize. She needs the security of knowing that you are willing to help her and invest in the growth of her life.

After you define the responsibilities in the home, it is your job to enforce them; don't make your wife enforce the duties. If it is your son's turn to clear the dishes from the table, then you should not encourage him to go play ball outside with you. You need to put your foot down and say, "Son, go do your duty." If you want to play ball or a game or watch a video with him, maybe you should help him clean off the table so that the two of you can get to it sooner. Your wife does not want to feel that she is the policeman of the house; you are that person. After a while a good woman will say, "Forget it. I will do it." Your family members won't learn to do their duties, and you will build a wall of resentment between you and your wife.

Marriages don't just go bad because of affairs. Marriages go bad because of neglectful, careless, unthinking, and unkind husbands. A wise husband who wants to fulfill his wife's needs will consider how to help her in her world. He will encourage her in her strengths and protect her from exposing her weaknesses. A wise husband will make the necessary investments to show his wife that he supports her duties in the marriage.

CHAPTER TEN

The Needs of Your Wife:

A Husband Who Can Handle Her Fears

*T*he fears of your wife are a test of your love. You must become aware of your wife's insecurities in order to remove her anxiety. You will learn those fears through her conversation; that is why conversation is essential to your marriage. Each wife has fears that are unique to her, but many women have these basic fears:

1. The insecurity of her husband's dying
2. Growing old
3. Becoming unattractive to her husband
4. Bad health
5. Complications due to past sins
6. Failing as a wife
7. Failing as a mother
8. Her husband's losing his job
9. Having a mental breakdown

10. Social awkwardness
11. Educational deficiencies
12. Physical safety when she is alone
13. The future of her children
14. Being displaced by another woman

You begin to provide securities from these fears through conversation. During a time of deep conversation, ask her how she really feels about one of those topics. Ask her point-blank when you are having a soul connection as you speak. When you are talking deeply, say, "I would like to talk about that fear." Your wife will hint at her fears. Allow me to illustrate how she hints and how you should respond.

Your wife hints about the fear of becoming unattractive. If your wife fears that she has become unattractive, she will not say, "I worry that I am not as attractive as I used to be." She might say, "I think I need to lose a little weight," or "I think I need to color my hair." Sometimes those might be vapid statements, but she is looking for more than a response that says, "Don't worry. You look fine!" Husbands make the mistake of not translating these statements into their native language of Husband. Your wife is looking to know if you are as attracted to her now as when you first noticed her. She wants to know if she is as pretty now as she was ten, eighteen, or twenty-six years ago.

A great response would be, "I think you are ten times prettier than when I met you. I thought you were beautiful 20 years ago, but I must have been half blind then because what you are now is absolutely gorgeous and stunning." You want to say things that are more than adequate and convince her that you are not going to hurt her in the area of her fear. When she fishes, you should fish back. The next step is to say, "There is something behind that question, and I want to talk about it. What is on your heart?"

The language of Wife has multiple layers of conversational talk. The more shallow level is where most wives converse with their husband, and it is the level that men misunderstand. A wife can be in front of a mirror fussing with her skirt because it doesn't properly drop over her hips and say, "I think I need to lose five pounds."

The shallow response from a husband is, "You do. In fact, you should go for ten."

If you respond, "You don't need to lose any weight," you are also responding incorrectly because in her heart she knows that she does, and she knows that you are not honest with her. Telling her that she doesn't need to lose any weight is equivalent to patting her on the head and saying, "What a good little girl you are." She is not looking for someone to pander to her. She is looking for someone to understand the statement.

Timing is essential in discussing sensitive matters. As the husband, you must discern when you can talk about them. If she is trying to get ready in a jiffy, she might say that she needs to lose weight out of frustration because nothing that she is trying on looks presentable. That is not the time to grab her by the shoulders and say, "In your deepest heart, what do you mean by that?" That method will not build intimate conversation with your wife. You don't talk about important matters as you are walking out the door or when she gets into the car when you are late.

Your wife fussed over how she looked before you met her. When you would meet for a date, she would try the clothes on, look in the mirror, and wonder if they fit in an attractive way. When the two of you would meet for a date, you would say, "Wow! You look beautiful. You are gorgeous!"

But you don't do that anymore, do you? Back then you were trying to draw her to you with your words. You were opening your heart and trying to connect it with hers. You used intimate words that told her how she stirred up your most intimate emotions. You couldn't wait to get married and have sex, and you grabbed her heart through the intimacy of your language. Now you're married, and the chase is done. You don't have to say those things anymore because you've got her. You will have a great marriage when you keep doing the same things that got her to like you in the first place.

Your wife wants to know where she fits in on your "fave-five" attraction list. She wants to know where she currently fits relative to when you were dating and falling in love. If she was willing to get married, then you must have sufficiently convinced her that she was attractive. She wants to know if she still measures up to the days of courtship.

Men blow off the romance once they get married. Men become fat and balding or gray-headed, and deep down they don't care like a woman cares about her body. Husbands make jokes such as, "You got it in the hips; I got it in the belly; we're just getting fat together." That is not romantic nor humorous material. She might laugh with you or jiggle with you, but inside she is wondering if you still find her attractive. The question has nothing to do with her weight because she isn't going to stay the same weight as when you married. Her fear is that you don't find her as attractive, and it hurts her to think that you may not.

Therein is the ultimate problem with pornography. Yes, it ruins your image of women, and it is lascivious, and it is perverse, and it is sinful, but the number-one problem that pornography will cause in your life is that it will destroy your wife's attitude of security.

Pornography tells your wife that she is not satisfying to you. When a man looks at pornography, he usually isn't looking at middle-aged whores unless he is extremely warped; he is looking at girls that are 18-to-25 years old. He wants to look at girls that have no lines or wrinkles. A wife then has to compete with a girl who is the age at which she dated her husband. The obvious question to her becomes, "Am I not as attractive as when I first met him?" She can't compete with the build of those ladies, and a wife's feelings of love and security are devastated.

Your wife hints about her fears of repercussions from past sins. If you married a woman who has a past of promiscuity, then she has embedded fears of retribution through future failures. Perhaps she was young and didn't realize how much it would hurt her. Perhaps she was deceived by a stud athlete or cowboy or a stud muffin in her hometown. She was a young girl who fell for a lie because she thought she would be accepted. Maybe she smoked dope, took other drugs, or was a drinker.

Once your wife came to her senses because of conviction or salvation, she wondered if God was going to judge her harshly in this life because of those sins. She would like to ask somebody, "Do you think God is going to judge me?" She wonders if those sins will haunt her in her old age. Your wife wonders if your 15-year-old son is having a difficult time because she slept with a boy when she was 15. She is wondering if she will reap what she sowed. Your wife won't ask you those questions because:

1. You may not know the answer.
2. You have similar doubts and fears.
3. You might be the boy with whom she slept when she was 15, and she doesn't want to hurt your feelings and spirit.
4. She is afraid that you will say, "Just get over it."

Your wife would like to ask someone, "Do you think it is going to matter?" No matter what the sin might be—even if it wasn't immorality—she likely carries some guilt with which she struggles.

When she is pouring out her heart about her fears of your teenage son or daughter entering puberty and adolescence, you should say, "I want you to tell me what you fear. Tell me your heart." As she bares her heart, she doesn't need a sermon or a lesson; she needs you to listen with your eyes and open up your heart and say, "I cannot tell you how glad I am that you shared your thoughts with me."

Your wife needs you to go back and review how God has blessed your life up to that moment. She needs you to wisely take the past and show how God has stepped into your lives and led you together, how He brought salvation to her, and how He worked all things together for good. She needs to know that you know how to take your past and show the grace of the Lord Jesus Christ and not show the judging hand of a wrathful God.

Your wife has a fear of growing old. Each Wednesday night at the First Baptist Church of Hammond, we take up an offering for someone in need. Sometimes the offerings are for missionaries who are leaving the mission field because of age or poor health. Their story might be that they have no insurance, and my church feels that it is our duty to take care of these veteran saints. If your wife hears a similar story and says, "I wonder how she is feeling about that" or "I feel bad for that lady," you should take it as a sign that she is wondering what will happen to her as she grows old. She is wondering what would happen to her if she were in that situation.

Provide the assurance to your wife that she will be cared for should you pass away. When she makes a statement about someone else's condition, you should grab her hand and say, "Be glad you married me. If I have a stroke or a heart attack, you are one rich cat. You are going to be well cared for." That statement should be true; you should have some type of insurance plan for her.

The space is not available to address every fear your wife might have. You need to recognize that your wife often expresses fear in a very lighthearted, cursory way. You must learn to hear what your wife is really wanting when she mentions certain issues. She wants to know that you care about her feelings. She wants to know that she is safe in expressing those to you. Ultimately, she wants to share herself with you in an intimately verbal expression. The key to her finding fulfillment in verbally connecting with you begins when you can ask at the appropriate time, "I hear what you are telling me, but what are your other feelings about that?"

Handle your wife's fears by asking God for wisdom in resolving them. Your prayer life needs to reflect that you understand your wife's needs. I often get asked what I pray because I am a pastor. People ask me if I pray for all of the missionaries by name and for everyone in my church. I tend to pray for people that I know are in trouble and people that have a specific need. I don't pray for general things; I don't pray for two thousand names each day. I don't have a list that I am trying to complete. I do pray for my wife, however.

When I pray for my wife, one of the things I pray for is for God to give me wisdom about her specific needs. I know what my wife's needs and fears are, so I pray for those; they are a vital part of my prayer life. A husband who doesn't know what his wife's needs and fears are can't begin to help her through prayer. If you don't know your wife's needs and fears, you should ask God to reveal those to you.

Many times a day I pray and beg God to tell me how to help her in a certain area. I ask Him for wisdom. I want to be the man that has the answers for my wife. Nothing pleases me more than when my wife says, "You made a statement some time ago when we were chatting that has really helped me." I get to see God answer my prayers in my relationship with my wife.

Are you praying that God will give you the wisdom to know how to handle or address the fears that your wife has? What Scripture can you give your wife for her problems? Do you know what steps of action you can take to help your wife? Beg God to give you the ability to provide security for your wife's fears.

CHAPTER ELEVEN

The Needs of Your Wife:

A Husband Who Loves Her

*A*s a man, you probably like that the Bible commands your wife to submit to you. In this chapter we are going to discuss what the Bible says about the love of a husband for his wife. The same Bible commands you to love your wife. This book has discussed many of the needs of your wife, but I have saved the greatest need for last. Your wife needs you to love her, so how much love do you have to give your wife?

"For the husband is the head of the wife, even as Christ is the head of the church: and he is the saviour of the body...Husbands, love your wives, even as Christ also loved the church, and gave himself for it; That he might sanctify and cleanse it with the washing of water by the word, That he might present it to himself a glorious church, not having spot, or wrinkle, or any such thing; but that it should be holy and without blemish." (Ephesians 5:23, 25-27)

Truthfully, husbands do not have enough love to give to their wives. If we look at the love that Christ has for the church, we will find that we are lacking in our love for our wives. We must figure out how we can provide the type of love that our wives need. Christ is your role model for loving your wife.

"The easiest, the most tempting, and the least creative response to conflict within an organization is to pretend it does not exist."

— Lyle E. Schaller

The Bible says a husband is to love as Christ loved. It is a lofty standard. Wives are only compared to the church, and it is a sinful organism. Husbands are compared to Christ Who is a perfect Being.

God did not say husbands love your wives as the church loves each other. Church members already do that. Some church people "love" their neighbor's wife and sleep with her occasionally if they can get by with it. Some church members "love" their neighbor's kids and fondle them if they can get by with it. Some members love breaking the law. Some church people "love" cheating their brothers and sisters out of money. Hiring lawyers, suing those who cheated them, and taking other church members to court is commonplace. Cheating, hurting, harming, fornicating, and committing adultery are ways some church members treat each other, so it would be easy to "love" our wives just like the people in churches "love" each other.

Fortunately for our wives, the Bible does use the church as the model for how husbands should love them. The standard for love is atmospherically lofty. The analogy is the wife as the human being and the husband as Christ. How do you love Christ? If you are like most people, you are weak in your love for Christ. You might be devoted one moment but be pulled by passion and lust and greed the next moment. We can praise God out of one side of our mouth and curse our brother with the other side. God knows the fickleness of humanity, so He tells us that our love for our wives must be beyond a normal human love.

As someone who studies the Bible, I want to close the Bible when I see that I have to have a Christlike love for my wife because that is impossible. I might as well quit. My wife gets off easy. All she has to do is submit to me as the church submits to Christ. The typical church doesn't submit to Christ, so a wife's submission isn't all that lofty. In our spiritual lives, we all look for reasons and excuses to do only what we have to do. We are not to love our wives only because we are commanded to. We must be willing to love them. We choose to love them just like Christ chose to save us.

A husband must give himself to his wife. Ephesians 5:25 says, *"Husbands, love your wives, even as Christ also loved the church, and gave himself for it."* You are the greatest gift your wife could ever receive. When Jesus gave Himself, He gave everything He had.

A common complaint that I hear from wives in a strained or weak marriage is, "My husband doesn't realize that I want him." For some strange reason, men don't catch that fact which they knew before they got married. She has always wanted you, and you once felt that you had to have her. After men get married, they are sprayed with a hypnotic dust that makes them avoid giving themselves to their new bride.

Affairs are comprised of two people who give themselves to each other. Affairs happen because people feel they can talk. There is an intense, romantic aura that is pervaded by two people who give themselves to each other; it is not just sex. For a woman, the biggest hurt of her husband's affair is not the sexual embrace, although that is staggering. The biggest hurt is that her husband didn't give himself to her during the time he spent with another woman.

Your wife doesn't get why she is no longer desirable. What your wife wants and needs is you, but you withdraw from her and you do not give all of you. That is as un-Christian as not tithing or committing adultery. A wife whose husband has completely given himself to her has never come to me for marriage counseling. She wants you—not your money, not your house, and not your car. You will not be rejected; she married you because she wants you.

Your wife wants all of you. That's why God commanded you to give yourself to her as Christ gave Himself. He gave His life, His pride, His dignity, and His material goods. Jesus gave everything, and so should you.

A husband must love his wife because his love sanctifies her. *Sanctify* means "to set her apart for yourself." Christ sanctified the church and has set believers apart for Himself. Christ sanctified the church through love, and you are to do the same for your wife. She needs to feel that she is one of a kind, singularly unique, and a prized possession. She will feel these ways to the degree that you love her.

Turmoil comes when a wife finds her husband looking elsewhere, wanting elsewhere, going elsewhere, and talking elsewhere. The elsewhere doesn't have to be another woman; the elsewhere can be anything. It could be a hobby, a craft, or a sport.

A husband must love his wife because his love cleanses her. Love cleanses; it purifies. Love will set your wife apart from lesser things. A wife who is preoccupied with material things is choosing a lesser thing than her husband. She becomes enthralled with material things when she is deprived of the much greater thing of her husband's love. Lesser things could be a cheap, tawdry sexual affair to escape the boredom of her own life, soap operas on television, trashy talk on the radio, gossip, and backbiting.

Newlyweds are happy people. They are not happy because they are anticipating the big house that they will someday occupy. They are happy because they have received each other.

My parents are an example of an older couple who were happy when they were together and poor, yet happy now that they are together and have a little money. The material goods never made a difference, but the love that my father had for my mother made her not want the lesser things. Those lesser things were anything other than her husband.

A husband shows his love through words. The Bible says that "...he [Christ] *might sanctify and cleanse it* [the church] *with the washing of water by the word.*" God showed His love to us by giving us His Word. The Bible says that the Word became flesh and dwelt among us. A wife craves to have her husband share words with her.

A common complaint that I hear from wives is that their husbands don't talk much to them. In Wife, this means that her husband doesn't love her much. You can say that you are not a talker, but you have to fix that. Your wife wants to hear you talk. She wants to hear what you have to say. She wants to hear what you have to say about her. A man comes home from work, and his wife says, "So tell me what your day was like."

"It was like every day. You ask me the same question every day. My day is like every day, end of discussion," he replies.

That is a horrible expression of love. There are over 880,000 words in the Bible; have you ever spoken that much to your wife? God wants you to love your wife through the words you use. Show her how uniquely special she is by the words you use. Set her apart as a one-of-a-kind person through the words you use.

Our words usually cause the opposite thing to happen than what we intended. When a man comes to me and says that his wife won't lose weight, smokes, drinks, goes to the gambling casino, talks too much with her friends, is addicted to her mother, or never talks to him, I always ask one thing. It is, "What words do you use to convince your wife that she is loved by you?"

He replies, "Well, when she puts on her clothes, I say, 'That is too tight; you need to lose a little weight.'"

"Is it working?" I ask, but he has no answer.

When Christ loved us, He demonstrated it. When a

lady was taken in adultery, He said, *"Neither do I con-demn thee: go, and sin no more."* When men nailed Him to a cross, He said, *"Father, forgive them; for they know not what they do."*

The typical man "loves" his wife with words by say-ing, "You are putting on a few extra pounds there; you better go see Weight Watchers. I will set the appoint-ment for you right now. Can I have a bag of chips? I am going to watch the ball game." Men are such hypocrites. We have love handles, and we tell our wives to lose weight. Our words are disapproving and crushing.

Smart men learn quickly that wives like lies. If a wife wants to know how she looks, the brilliant man says, "Have you gone on a diet? You look great in that outfit. Come here and let me get a hold of that." He hugs her and touches her and feels around and says, "You have lost weight, haven't you? I am so impressed. Wow." A wife would kill for a husband like that.

A husband's love cleanses a wife from sin and defilement. If your wife has some big or little faults, you help her with those by loving her. *Cleanse* means "to wash away the defilement or the sin or the wickedness." God loved you so much that it made you righteous. His love solved every sin problem of mine. I am so loved that I am considered on the same level as Jesus Christ in the sight of the Father. Love transforms a person from common and ordinary to extraordinary and uncommon.

When a person feels loved, he or she soars way up above the stars and reaches a level he/she could never have reached before. When she believes in me, I can do anything. The man who has a woman who believes in him can do anything. When a man loves a woman, she feels that she is one-of-a-kind, and she would walk away from sin for her man.

A husband's love delivers his wife from guilt. *Cleanse* means "to deliver from guilt." When a man loves his wife, his love takes away mistakes of the past. The Bible says that you are the savior to the body of marriage. Your wife is not the savior; you are. If the wife was called a savior, it would be a bad symbol because it would imply that she could save herself; that is wicked theology.

The theology taught in that passage is that the woman needs a savior. Mankind cannot save himself; he needs a Saviour. God showcases that analogy in a marriage. The woman cannot save herself from her problems, but the husband saves her from them.

Savior is a unique term. It does mean that you are a deliverer or a helper or a rescuer, but all those words imply something. When you are rescued, the implication is that you were in danger or trouble. You don't want to be rescued from a good situation. When your wife is in a position where she could not help herself, your love pulls her out.

Your wife needs you to be a human, God-like individual who makes her feel that her mistakes don't matter to you. God erased your mistakes. As the husband, you are to make sure that you love your wife despite her mistakes and that you never bring them up.

There is a story of a husband and a wife who decided they needed to improve their marriage. They read marriage books, listened to CDs, and finally decided on a particular method for improving their marriage. The wife said, "For each day of the month, I will write down all the things I think are mistakes that you have made. I won't tell them to you; I will merely write them down and put them in a shoe box. Each day I will write the things on a new piece of paper. I won't say anything bad about you; I won't harp about it; I won't nag. At the end of the thirty days, you will open the box and read them so that you can work on them. You do the same for me. We will each have our own box into which we put our gripes."

He said, "Okay, I will do that too. Every time I see a mistake of yours and every time I see a fault or an error, I will write down the mistake and the error on the piece of paper. After thirty days, you can read them."

She said, "Let's do it."

When the 30 days were finished, both boxes were stuffed full. The husband opened his box and found 30 pieces of paper each with a litany of wrongdoings. He hadn't away put his socks and underwear. He hadn't hung up his coat. He didn't put dishes in the sink. He didn't park the car properly in the driveway. The garage was messy. He didn't say "I love you" enough times. He had 30 pieces of paper that railed against his character.

She said, "What do you think?"

He graciously said, "I will work on them."

He handed her his box. The first piece of paper that she opened said "I love you." The second piece of paper said "I love you." The third piece of paper through the thirtieth piece of paper said "I love you." The 30 pieces of paper all said the same thing.

"Are you being funny?" she asked.

"No," he replied. "Every time I saw a mistake, I realized that I just needed to love you, so I wrote that down."

The only cure for a wife's mistake is a husband's love. When Jesus Christ saw you and me sinning, there was no way to fix it. He simply said, "I so love the world." A wife who has that kind of love from her husband has unlimited freedom to rise to the level of the lover. I am allowed to sit on a throne with God and rule as a king and a priest because of Jesus Christ's love.

God has not zapped me. He hasn't given me electric shock therapy. He hasn't scrubbed me down with lye, and He hasn't washed my mouth out with soap. God has only and always loved me. When I am convinced and aware of the love of Christ toward me, it cleanses me and brings me up to a whole new level of living.

Your challenge is the same. You must love your wife through her mistakes and flaws. Husband, you are commanded to love her. God told you to love her because He made her in need of love. You were the man who said that you would meet that need, and she needs you to be that man you promised her to be at the wedding altar. Will you start being that man today?

Do you have a better understanding of her language? Do you understand that you do not express yourself in the same manner as your wife? As the leader of your home, it is your job to understand what she is saying when she speaks to you. As her husband, you are commanded to love her. Fulfill your roles as a husband and help her fulfill her roles as a wife. As you accept and fulfill your roles which God designed, you will function more effectively in those roles and better translate and interpret the words and needs of your wife.